Praying for Israel and the Jewish people in the last days

Lindsay Hassall

GILEAD
B O O K S
PUBLISHING

First published in Great Britain, July 2018
Reprinted September 2019

www.GileadBooksPublishing.com

2 4 6 8 10 9 7 5 3 1

British Library Cataloguing-in-Publication Data:
A catalogue record for this book is available from the British
Library.

ISBN: 978-1-9997224-6-3

Cover design: Nathan Ward

Introduction

This book began just as I finished my time of prayer one day. For seven days I had been praying for the peace of Jerusalem and the Jews. Each day I wrote my prayers down to help me focus and think through what I was praying and why. I took a passage of scripture and meditated on it so that my prayers were in line with God's will. When I had finished I heard the voice of his Holy Spirit say to my spirit to extend the seven-day devotional prayer for a month. This book is the product of that month, where I was focusing prayer each day on Jerusalem and God's people the Jews.

My prayer and hope is that you will find this book useful to assist you in praying for the Jews. It is an aid, a springboard to help you, to inspire you, to give you ideas of what to pray for.

It is important that we pray for the peace of Jerusalem. King David said we are to:

Pray for the peace of Jerusalem! (Psalm 122:6)

The CUFI (Christians United For Israel) website states that "This year, Israel celebrates its 70th birthday. The survival of the Jewish people, the revival of their ancient language, and their return to their ancestral land is one of the greatest miracles in recorded history."

As I re-read Day 29 there was a drone invasion of Israel's air space launched by one of her neighbours.

Israel, Jerusalem, all Jews everywhere need our prayers and our support.

Sadly, many Christians do not pray for Jerusalem. Some, even speak against it. To these people I would say:

> And when he [Jesus] drew near and saw the city, he wept over it. (Luke 19:41)

Jesus wept over Jerusalem, so can we as his followers not pray for what touches his heart?

Lindsay

Day 1

Psalm 122:1-9 A Song of ascents. Of David.

[1] I was glad when they said to me, "Let us go to the house of the LORD!"

[2] Our feet have been standing within your gates, O Jerusalem!

[3] Jerusalem   built as a city that is bound firmly together,

[4] to which the tribes go up, the tribes of the LORD, as was decreed for Israel, to give thanks to the name of the LORD.

[5] There thrones for judgment were set, the thrones of the house of David.

[6] Pray for the peace of Jerusalem! "May they be secure who love you!

[7] Peace be within your walls and security within your towers!"

[8] For my brothers and companions' sake I will say, "Peace be within you!"

[9] For the sake of the house of the LORD our God, I will seek your good.

Father,
I pray for the peace of Jerusalem.
I pray for peace within its walls.

I pray for peace in the homes of all who live in Jerusalem especially the homes of those in positions of leadership and influence within Jerusalem.

I pray that there will be prosperity within the homes of all who live in Jerusalem.

I decree and declare peace over Jerusalem.

I decree and declare that Jerusalem will be a place where your people may give thanks to you, may worship you and be in your presence in freedom and peace.

Father,

Show me ways I can seek the good of Jerusalem.

Show me ways I can do good to all who live in Jerusalem.

Show me ways I can support and strengthen your city.

Father,

I pray that the earthly Jerusalem will reflect the Heavenly Jerusalem.

I pray that the earthly Jerusalem will manifest the Kingdom of God.

Father,

I ask these things in the name of your Son, The Messiah of Jerusalem, Jesus the King of Jerusalem.

Amen.

Day 2

Genesis 12:1-3

[1] Now the LORD said to Abram, "Go from your country and your kindred and your father's house to the land that I will show you.

[2] And I will make of you a great nation, and I will bless you and make your name great, so that you will be a blessing.

[3] I will bless those who bless you, and him who dishonors you I will curse, and in you all the families of the earth shall be blessed."

Father,
I thank you that you called Abram to the Land of Israel.
I thank you that he was willing to sacrifice everything to obey you and receive your gift.

Father,
you promised to make Abram into a great nation.
Enable and empower Israel to be great in your eyes.
Enable and empower Israel to be great in the eyes of other nations, the nations of the world.

Father,
you blessed Abram

Father, continue to bless the descendants of Abraham through his son Isaac, so that they may be a blessing to all peoples everywhere and to all the nations of the world.

Father,
your people are precious in your sight.
How I treat them affects how you treat me.
I decree and declare that
I will bless your people.
I will do good to your people.
I will always speak well of your people.
I decree and declare that
I will not wrong your people.
I will not speak evil about your people.
I will not curse your people.

Father,
When your people sin against you or against other people I will pray for them.
I will pray that you will forgive them.
I will pray that you will open the eyes of their hearts to act only in love, righteousness and peace towards other people.

I ask these things in the name of Jesus, the Prince of Peace, the Son of Righteousness, the Son of Love.
Amen.

Day 3

> **2 Corinthians 3:14**
>
> [14] But their minds were hardened. For to this day, when they read the old covenant, that same veil remains unlifted, because only through Christ is it taken away.

Father,

When Jesus was with his disciples he opened up their hearts to see who he was from the scriptures.

> [25] And he said to them, "O foolish ones, and slow of heart to believe all that the prophets have spoken! [26] Was it not necessary that the Christ should suffer these things and enter into His glory?"
> [27] And beginning with Moses and all the Prophets, he interpreted to them in all the Scriptures the things concerning himself. (Luke 24:25-27)
> [32] They said to each other, "Did not our hearts burn within us while he talked to us on the road, while he opened to us the Scriptures?" (Luke 24:32)

Father,

I pray for your people.

Their minds are blinded as they read the scriptures so that they are unable to see that Moses and the other prophets reveal how Jesus sacrificed his life for them, his people, and that your Son, Jesus Christ of Nazareth is their Messiah and their soon coming King.

Father,
As your people read the Old Testament and hear your Word read in their synagogues I pray that
your Holy Spirit will open the eyes of their hearts
your Holy Spirit will remove the veil that is over their minds
I pray that your Holy Spirit will
Inspire them as they read and listen.
Teach them as they think and meditate.
Correct their thinking about your Son.
Instruct them how to receive Jesus as their Saviour, their Messiah, their King.

In the name of Jesus, I decree and declare that all the strongholds Satan has over their minds are pulled down and in the name of Jesus I decree and declare that the veil over their minds is lifted by the Glory of God, that same Glory that raised Jesus from the dead.

Father,
Soften the hearts of your people towards your Son, their Messiah.
Amen

Day 4

> **Genesis 18:19**
>
> [19] For I have chosen him, that he may command his children and his household after him to keep the way of the LORD by doing righteousness and justice, so that the LORD may bring to Abraham what he has promised him."

Father,

you chose to bless Abraham and to give to him what you had promised. I thank you that this is still true for today. Today, the Jews are still your chosen people. Today, you still want to bless them. Today, your promises still stand true for them.

Father,

Abraham was the father that you needed to enable his children to experience your blessing in their lives.

Father, I pray for all Jewish fathers.

May they understand the revelation that they are chosen

May they teach and guide their children, so that they and their families may keep your way, may obey your word, may obey your voice which still speaks to them.

Father,
I pray also for all Rabbi's.
May they faithfully teach their students
to be obedient to you
to establish justice and righteousness

May all Jews in Israel and throughout the world so love you and their neighbours that you always bless them and never discipline them.

May they know you as their father, may they know your holiness and righteousness, your love and mercy as Abraham did.

May they always be blessed as Abraham was.

Amen

Day 5

Isaiah 62:1-3

1 For Zion's sake I will not keep silent, and for Jerusalem's sake I will not be quiet, until her righteousness goes forth as brightness, and her salvation as a burning torch.

2 The nations shall see your righteousness, and all the kings your glory, and you shall be called by a new name that the mouth of the LORD will give.

3 you shall be a crown of beauty in the hand of the LORD, and a royal diadem in the hand of your God.

Isaiah 62:11-12

11 Behold, the LORD has proclaimed to the end of the earth: Say to the daughter of Zion, "Behold, your salvation comes; behold, his reward is with him, and his recompense before him."

12 And they shall be called The Holy People, The Redeemed of the LORD; and you shall be called Sought Out, A City Not Forsaken.

Father,

I come before you as Isaiah did, unable to keep quiet about your people and about Jerusalem.

For the sake of Jerusalem, I will pray.

For the sake of all who live in that city and also in the land of Israel I will pray.

I will pray until the Jews are a crown of beauty in your hand once more.

Father, your people have a calling from you on their lives that they are to fulfil.

Father, your desire is for Israel and Jerusalem and for all your people everywhere to be glorious before you so that they will affect this world.

Father,

I pray for your people whether they reside in Israel or throughout the world.

May your people walk and live in the covenant you have with them.

May they be obedient to your laws and your voice.

May they be restored so that righteousness will flow from them as individuals, as a nation and as a government so that they are a light to all others.

Restore your people so that others may see your righteousness and holiness living and abiding in them.

Restore your people so that others may see your presence and your glory upon your people.

Father,
Through your Holy Spirit restore the hearts of your people to you.
Through the Law speak to your people.
So that they may become what you have declared your holy people,
your redeemed people.
A people that others are proud to be associated with.
A people not forsaken by their God.

Father,
your people are waiting for their Messiah, your Son.
When he comes may he bring them rewards and not judgements.

We pray this in the name of your Son, our Saviour, their Messiah, Jesus.

Amen

Day 6

Psalms 121:1-8

[1] A Song of Ascents. I lift up my eyes to the hills. From where does my help come?

[2] My help comes from the LORD, who made heaven and earth.

[3] He will not let your foot be moved; he who keeps you will not slumber.

[4] Behold, he who keeps Israel will neither slumber nor sleep.

[5] The LORD is your keeper; the LORD is your shade on your right hand.

[6] The sun shall not strike you by day, nor the moon by night.

[7] The LORD will keep you from all evil; he will keep your life.

[8] The LORD will keep your going out and your coming in from this time forth and forevermore.

Father,

Just as your people sang this Psalm as they travelled to Jerusalem as pilgrims to celebrate and worship before you at your appointed feasts before the Fall of Jerusalem, I ask that all Jews today travelling from amongst the nations to Israel and those living in the Land will also be inspired to look to you, and only to you, for their help. For the wisdom, knowledge, understanding, guidance and strength they need as individuals and as a nation.

Father,
I ask that this is not just a song of worship on their lips but is also the song of dedication that rises from their hearts each moment of each day.

Father,
I lift my eyes to you to pray for your people.
May your people whether in Israel or in the world always look to you for help, wisdom and guidance.
May your people always hear your voice.
May your people always understand and always know your commands and your will.
And may your people always be obedient to all that you have said and written.
Protect and guard your people so that they do not stumble.
Protect them so that they remain faithful to you in their hearts and lives.

Father,
We pray for your people as Jesus taught us to pray for ourselves,
'Deliver them from evil'.

Father,

Preserve your people so that the spirit of anti-Semitism does not harm or destroy them.

We ask this as you are their Shepherd.

Amen.

Day 7

Ezekiel 43:1-9

1 Then he led me to the gate, the gate facing east.

2 And behold, the glory of the God of Israel was coming from the east. And the sound of his coming was like the sound of many waters, and the earth shone with his glory.

3 And the vision I saw was just like the vision that I had seen when he came to destroy the city, and just like the vision that I had seen by the Chebar canal. And I fell on my face.

4 As the glory of the LORD entered the temple by the gate facing east,

5 the Spirit lifted me up and brought me into the inner court; and behold, the glory of the LORD filled the temple.

6 While the man was standing beside me, I heard one speaking to me out of the temple,

7 and he said to me, "Son of man, this is the place of my throne and the place of the soles of my feet, where I will dwell in the midst of the people of Israel forever.

> And the house of Israel shall no more defile my holy name, neither they, nor their kings, by their whoring and by the dead bodies of their kings at their high places,
>
> 8 by setting their threshold by my threshold and their doorposts beside my doorposts, with only a wall between me and them. They have defiled my holy name by their abominations that they have committed, so I have consumed them in my anger.
>
> 9 Now let them put away their whoring and the dead bodies of their kings far from me, and I will dwell in their midst forever.

Father,

Your Glory filled the tabernacle and then the temple until the disobedience and the unfaithfulness of your people caused your Glory to leave. Ezekiel saw your Glory leave the temple, but he also saw and prophesied the return of your Glory.

Father,

I pray for the day when the Glory of your presence will return in all its fullness to your people, to your nation.

I pray that the Temple will be rebuilt and that the Temple Mount will once again become the place where they worship you and honour your name.

I pray that your people will have such a reverence for you and your name that they will never again disregard your voice, reject your prophets nor disobey your word.

I pray that your people will never again bring dishonour to your name, your presence, or your glory. I pray that they will welcome your Son as their Saviour and Messiah.

I pray that they will welcome your Son as their King and their Shepherd.

Amen.

Day 8

Isaiah 54:15-17

15 If anyone stirs up strife, it is not from me; whoever stirs up strife with you shall fall because of you.

16 Behold, I have created the smith who blows the fire of coals and produces a weapon for its purpose. I have also created the ravager to destroy;

17 no weapon that is fashioned against you shall succeed, and you shall refute every tongue that rises against you in judgment. This is the heritage of the servants of the LORD and their vindication from me, declares the LORD."

Father,
Anti-Semitism of any kind is not from you nor is it at any time your will for your people.

Father,
The 'Smith' and the 'Ravager' are part of your heavenly creation to work in this world to protect your people and to destroy any weapon that is forged and created to bring harm, destruction or death to your people.

Father,

Release the weapon that the 'Smith' has created to destroy anti-Semitism.

Father,

Release the 'Ravager' to use the weapon the 'Smith' has created to destroy all weapons of harm created to harm your people.

Father,

I pray for your people.
Satan's will for your people is death and destruction, your will for your people is life, health and prosperity.

Father,

I pray that your will be done on this earth as it is done in heaven.

Father,

I decree and declare that your will be done amongst your people.

Father,

I pray that no weapon that Satan has created or will ever begin to create against your people will ever succeed.

Father,

I decree and declare that no weapon that Satan forms against Israel and your people will succeed.

I decree and declare that anyone who speaks against Israel or any of your people will be silenced and condemned by you.

This is their right because they belong to you.

This is their heritage because they are your people.

Father,

I thank you that their righteousness comes from you and not from their acts of obedience to your voice and your law.

May all your people believe in and accept your gift of righteousness to them.

May all your people believe in and accept the gift of your Son to them.

Amen

Day 9

> **Numbers 6:22-27**
>
> [22] The LORD spoke to Moses, saying,
>
> [23] Speak to Aaron and his sons, saying, Thus you shall bless the people of Israel: you shall say to them,
>
> [24] The LORD bless you and keep you;
>
> [25] the LORD make his face to shine upon you and be gracious to you;
>
> [26] the LORD lift up his countenance upon you and give you peace.
>
> [27] "So shall they put my name upon the people of Israel, and I will bless them."

Father,

My desire, my heart is to bless Israel and to bless your people, the children of Israel, regardless of where they live, in the Land or out of the Land.

Father,

Bless them.

Prosper them.

Empower them to be successful.

Father,

Keep them.

Protect them.
Preserve them.

Father,
Make your face to shine upon them.
Enlighten them.

Father,
Be gracious to them.
Be kind to them.
Be merciful to them.
Give favour to them.

Father,
Lift up your countenance upon them.
Show them your approval.

Father,
Give them peace.
Give them prosperity.
Give them health.

Father,
I put your name on your children, the children of Israel,
so you will bless them.

Father,
As I bless with my words give me opportunities to also
bless by my actions. Thank you, Father, for your
promises and your word. Amen.

Day 10

> **Matthew 18:18**
>
> [18] Truly, I say to you, whatever you bind on earth shall be bound in heaven, and whatever you loose on earth shall be loosed in heaven.

Father,
Your Son, a Jew, one of the children of Israel, said these words.

Father,
I do not want any of my words to bring a curse upon the nation of Israel.
I want to only speak words that will bless them.
I do not want my words to bind or restrict your children in what you have called them to do.
I do not want my words to bind or restrict your children so they are hindered from entering into the place they have in your plan and your will for them in these last days.
I do not want my negative comments to affect their reputation or their ability to be your separated ones, your holy ones.

Father,

Forgive me for anything that I may have said that is not supportive of, nor in favour of your people.

Forgive me for anything that I may have said that has proven not to be a blessing to them.

I decree and declare that all my words will be a blessing to Israel and to your people.

I decree and declare that all my words will enable them to be your people in all their fullness with your fullness residing in their midst.

I decree and declare that all the words I utter will empower and enable Israel to be a light to all nations.

I decree and declare that all the words I utter will empower and enable your people to be faithful to you, to be edified by you and be built up in their most holy faith.

In the name of your Son I make these prayers, these decrees, these declarations.

Amen.

Day 11

Zechariah 2:8

8 For thus said the LORD of hosts, after his glory sent me to the nations who plundered you, for he who touches you touches the apple of his eye:

Deuteronomy 32:9-12

9 But the LORD's portion is his people, Jacob his allotted heritage.

10 "He found him in a desert land, and in the howling waste of the wilderness; he encircled him, he cared for him, he kept him as the apple of his eye.

11 Like an eagle that stirs up its nest, that flutters over its young, spreading out its wings, catching them, bearing them on its pinions,

Father,
your people, your nation, Israel is the apple of your eye.
They are special to you.
They are your favourite nation and your favoured nation in all the world.

Out of all the peoples in the world they are your chosen ones.

Father,
I thank you for what you have done for your people.
you found them
you led them
you kept them
you provided for them.
And Father, I thank you that you still do all these things for your precious people today.

Father,
your Son whilst he was living in Israel said, referring to the other nations:

> 40 And the King will answer them, 'Truly, I say to you, as you did it to one of the least of these my brothers, you did it to me.' (Matthew 25:40)

> 45 Then he will answer them, saying, 'Truly, I say to you, as you did not do it to one of the least of these, you did not do it to me.' (Matthew 25:45)

Father,
Whatever I do to any of your people I do to you.
Whatever I do not do to any of your people I do not do to you.

Father,

I decree and declare that from this day forward I will bless and seek to be a blessing to your people and to the nation you have called and chosen to be your own.

Father,

May all peoples of all nations also do only good to Israel and to the Jews.

Thank you, Father.

Amen.

Day 12

Joel 2:28-3:1

28 "And it shall come to pass afterward, that I will pour out my Spirit on all flesh; your sons and your daughters shall prophesy, your old men shall dream dreams, and your young men shall see visions.

29 Even on the male and female servants in those days I will pour out my Spirit.

30 "And I will show wonders in the heavens and on the earth, blood and fire and columns of smoke.

31 The sun shall be turned to darkness, and the moon to blood, before the great and awesome day of the LORD comes.

32 And it shall come to pass that everyone who calls on the name of the LORD shall be saved. For in Mount Zion and in Jerusalem there shall be those who escape, as the LORD has said, and among the survivors shall be those whom the LORD calls.

3:1 "For behold, in those days and at that time, when I restore the fortunes of Judah and Jerusalem.

Father,

I pray that what the body of Jesus, his Church, experienced at Pentecost your people and your nation will also experience.

Father,

Pour out your Holy Spirit afresh onto your people.

I pray that your people will be once again a prophetic people to this world.

Father,

Pour out your Holy Spirit afresh onto your people.

I pray that you will raise up amongst your people men like Samuel and women like Deborah who can speak your Word into your people and your nation.

Father,

Pour out your Holy Spirit afresh onto your people.

Give to your people dreams and visions.

So that they have a fresh understanding of you, your name and your Kingdom.

So that they have the eyes of their hearts enlightened.

So they may fulfil your calling and plan in these last days.

So that they may understand their heritage with you.

So that they may understand their future with you.

Father,

Pour out your Holy Spirit afresh onto your people.

I pray that your people will call upon you, your name, and be delivered from any judgement.
I pray that your people will call upon you, your name, and be delivered from all destruction.

Father,
Pour out your Holy Spirit afresh onto your people so that the fortunes of Israel may be restored.

Father,
Pour out your Holy Spirit afresh onto your people in the name of Jesus, whom you sent to save your people from their sins.

Amen.

Day 13

Isaiah 11:1-5

1 There shall come forth a shoot from the stump of Jesse, and a branch from his roots shall bear fruit.

2 And the Spirit of the LORD shall rest upon him, the Spirit of wisdom and understanding, the Spirit of counsel and might, the Spirit of knowledge and the fear of the LORD.

3 And his delight shall be in the fear of the LORD. He shall not judge by what his eyes see, or decide disputes by what his ears hear,

4 but with righteousness he shall judge the poor, and decide with equity for the meek of the earth; and he shall strike the earth with the rod of his mouth, and with the breath of his lips he shall kill the wicked.

5 Righteousness shall be the belt of his waist, and faithfulness the belt of his loins.

Father,

Pour out your Holy Spirit onto your people as you did on the Church on the day of Pentecost.

Father, your people need your Spirit.

They need .

The Spirit of Wisdom.

The Spirit of Understanding.

The Spirit of Counsel.

The Spirit of Might.

The Spirit of Knowledge.

The Spirit of the fear of you.

Father,

Empower your people through your Holy Spirit so that all those in Israel in positions of authority, the Prime Minister and all those who serve in Government, all those who are in positions of authority in the military, may discern and judge not with their natural human senses but with the wisdom, knowledge and insight from your Holy Spirit so that all their dealings are in righteousness and reflect their faithfulness and closeness to you.

Father,

May all your people be girded with righteousness and faithfulness.

Father,

forgive your people for grieving your Holy Spirit and for not keeping in step with your Holy Spirit in the past. May they not be guilty of this again in the future.

Father,

I ask this in the name of Jesus who was from his birth filled with your Holy Spirit and at his baptism was empowered by your Holy Spirit for ministry and at his death was raised up by your Holy Spirit.

Amen.

Day 14

Isaiah 58:6-8

6 "Is not this the fast that I choose: to loose the bonds of wickedness, to undo the straps of the yoke, to let the oppressed go free, and to break every yoke?

7 Is it not to share your bread with the hungry and bring the homeless poor into your house; when you see the naked, to cover him, and not to hide yourself from your own flesh?

8 Then shall your light break forth like the dawn, and your healing shall spring up speedily; your righteousness shall go before you; the glory of the LORD shall be your rear guard.

Father,

I pray for your people living in the Land of Israel.

I pray for the Government, the Knesset.

I pray for all those in positions of authority in Israel who work in:

Government.

The military.

Universities.

Businesses.

Schools.

I ask that they will seek you.

I ask that they will be eager to know your ways.

I ask that as a nation they will know what is right and always do right.

I ask that they will not forsake your commandments to them.

I ask that they will humble themselves before you.

I ask that they will always seek your face.

I ask that they will always listen to your voice and obey it.

Father,

I pray that they will.

Loose the chains of injustice.

Untie the cords of any yoke holding them back from hearing and obeying your voice .

Set the oppressed free.

Break every yoke of bondage holding them in darkness.

Share their food with the hungry.

Provide shelter for the homeless.

Clothe the naked.

Have their eyes opened to the needs of those under their authority.

Father,

I pray for Israel and the Knesset.

May your light break forth in their hearts and their midst

May your healing come to their lives, hearts, bodies and nation.
May their righteousness be known amongst the nations.
May your glory be seen upon them.

Father,
May you always be their guide.
May you always be their strength.
May you always be their restorer.
May you always be their joy.

Amen.

Day 15

Isaiah 52:13-53:6

13 Behold, my servant shall act wisely; he shall be high and lifted up, and shall be exalted.

14 As many were astonished at you—his appearance was so marred, beyond human semblance, and his form beyond that of the children of mankind—

15 so shall he sprinkle many nations. Kings shall shut their mouths because of him, for that which has not been told them they see, and that which they have not heard they understand.

53:1 Who has believed what he has heard from us? And to whom has the arm of the LORD been revealed?

2 For he grew up before him like a young plant, and like a root out of dry ground; he had no form or majesty that we should look at him, and no beauty that we should desire him.

3 He was despised and rejected by men, a man of sorrows and acquainted with grief; and as one from whom men hide their faces he was despised, and we esteemed him not.

> 4 Surely he has borne our griefs and carried our sorrows; yet we esteemed him stricken, smitten by God, and afflicted.
>
> 5 But he was pierced for our transgressions; he was crushed for our iniquities; upon him was the chastisement that brought us peace, and with his wounds we are healed.
>
> 6 All we like sheep have gone astray; we have turned—every one—to his own way; and the LORD has laid on him the iniquity of us all.

Father,

I pray that your people will see that Jesus is your servant who came to serve them, to free them and not to condemn them.

I pray that your people will see that Jesus, the man who was despised, rejected and crucified is alive today and is still your servant whose desire is to still come to them to serve them, to free them and not to condemn them.

Father,

May your people receive the revelation that Jesus is the one who:

Has borne their grief.

Carried their sorrows.

Was wounded for their transgressions.

Was bruised for their iniquities.

Bore the chastisement that brings them peace, Shalom.

By his stripes, they are healed.

Father,

May your people receive the revelation that although they have strayed from you their Shepherd you have laid the sin of their straying on your servant, your own Son, so that they may be restored fully to you and experience your love and your care in all its fullness once again in their lives, families and nation.

We ask these things in the name of Jesus, whose name means, 'He will save his people from their sins'. (Matthew 1:21)

Amen

Day 16

> **Psalms 23:1-6**
>
> [1] A Psalm of David. The LORD is my shepherd; I shall not want.
>
> [2] He makes me lie down in green pastures. He leads me beside still waters.
>
> [3] He restores my soul. He leads me in paths of righteousness for his name's sake.
>
> [4] Even though I walk through the valley of the shadow of death, I will fear no evil, for you are with me; your rod and your staff, they comfort me.
>
> [5] You prepare a table before me in the presence of my enemies; you anoint my head with oil; my cup overflows.
>
> [6] Surely goodness and mercy shall follow me all the days of my life, and I shall dwell in the house of the LORD forever.

Father,

I thank you that you are a Shepherd not just to your nation, Israel, but also Shepherd to all Jews living throughout the nations.

They are your flock. The people of your pasture. The sheep of your hand.

They are the people you love and care for.
They are the people you protect and lead.

Father,
I thank you that because you are their Shepherd then.
They shall not be in want.
You make them lie down in green pastures.
You shall lead them beside still waters.
You shall restore their souls.
You shall lead them in paths of righteousness for your
name's sake.

And Father, I rejoice that when they go through difficult
times you will not leave them and
as they walk through the valley of the shadow of death.
They need not fear any evil for
you are with them
your rod and your staff will comfort them.

And Father, I thank you that when they are persecuted
and threatened.
You prepare a table before them in the presence of
their enemies.
You anoint them with oil.
Their cups run over.

Father, I thank you that Israel is precious to you and
that,

your mercy and your goodness shall follow them all the days of their lives and
they shall dwell in your house for ever.

Father
I pray that all the people in the nation as well as the leaders of the nation will,
honour you as their Shepherd,
Follow you as their Shepherd.
Listen to you as their Shepherd.

Father,
I pray also that they will receive the revelation that their Shepherd laid down the life of his Son for them.

Jesus,
I thank you that you are the Good Shepherd and you laid down your life for your people, for your nation.

Amen

Day 17

Isaiah 9:6-7

[6] For to us a child is born, to us a son is given; and the government shall be upon his shoulder, and his name shall be called Wonderful Counselor, Mighty God, Everlasting Father, Prince of Peace.

[7] Of the increase of his government and of peace there will be no end, on the throne of David and over his kingdom, to establish it and to uphold it with justice and with righteousness from this time forth and forevermore. The zeal of the LORD of hosts will do this.

Father,
your Son came to establish your kingdom rule and reign on this earth in all its fullness.
What David began, Jesus came to finish.
What Isaiah prophesied, Jesus came to fulfil.

Father,
I thank you that this is your will and your zeal will ensure your will is done. No-one and nothing can stop this happening.

I join my prayers to your zeal and pray that these things will come to pass.

Father,
I thank you that you prophesied to your people through Isaiah that a child would be born and a son would be given to your people.

Father,
I thank you that you gave your Son to your people.
I thank you that your Son was the child born in Bethlehem to fulfil the prophecies about the promised Messiah.

Father,
I pray for your people.
May they see that Jesus is the one whom Isaiah talked about.
Open their eyes so that they may see that Jesus fulfilled the prophetic words in these verses.

Father,
I thank you that the government of your people, the government of Israel, the government of your Kingdom on this earth rests on his shoulders.
I pray that your people will receive and obey your Son so that they may experience his leadership and covering, so that they may experience true peace, Shalom, in their lives, families and nation.

Jesus,

I thank you that you are the,

Wonderful Counsellor to your people.

The Mighty God who loves them.

The Everlasting Father who protects them.

The Prince of Peace who rules over them.

Amen.

Day 18

Isaiah 41:8-10

8 But you, Israel, my servant, Jacob, whom I have chosen, the offspring of Abraham, my friend;

9 you whom I took from the ends of the earth, and called from its farthest corners, saying to you, "you are my servant, I have chosen you and not cast you off";

10 fear not, for I am with you; be not dismayed, for I am your God; I will strengthen you, I will help you, I will uphold you with my righteous right hand.

Father,

you chose Abraham, Isaac and Jacob and their descendants to be your chosen people for one purpose and that was to serve you.

Father,

May your people be obedient to your purpose and calling for them.

Father,

I pray that your people will honour, revere and obey you as their God, King and Master.

I pray that your nation and each member of that nation whether they live in the Israel or in other parts of the world amongst the nations of the world will seek to

Obey you.

Hear your voice.

Put you first in all things.

Honour the Sabbath.

Listen to your prophets.

Study your Word.

Pray to you.

Father,

You have said "I have chosen thee, and not cast thee away".

Manifest yourself to your people in ways that they understand so that they know you are still the God of Israel and that you are still their Shepherd.

Demonstrate your love to them so that your people will cling to you for life and so that the nations of the world will respect and honour your servant nation.

> 23 For the LORD will pass through to strike the Egyptians, and when he sees the blood on the lintel and on the two doorposts, the LORD will pass over the door and will not allow the destroyer to enter your houses to strike you. (Exodus 12:23)

When the blood was applied to the doors of your servants houses you entered in to protect the destroyer from entering in to take their lives.

Your Son shed his blood for this world. He died as the Lamb of God to take away the sins of this world. your nation is part of this world.

Father,
Enter into the homes of all your people so that Satan may not enter in to steal, kill and destroy lives and families.

We ask this in the name of the one whose blood is in heaven and speaks louder than the blood of Abel and all the martyred ones, the name of Jesus.

Amen.

Day 19

Luke 24:44-49

44 Then he said to them, "These are my words that I spoke to you while I was still with you, that everything written about me in the Law of Moses and the Prophets and the Psalms must be fulfilled."

45 Then he opened their minds to understand the Scriptures,

46 and said to them, "Thus it is written, that the Christ should suffer and on the third day rise from the dead,

47 and that repentance for the forgiveness of sins should be proclaimed in his name to all nations, beginning from Jerusalem.

48 you are witnesses of these things.

49 And behold, I am sending the promise of my Father upon you. But stay in the city until you are clothed with power from on high."

Acts 10:42-44

42 And he commanded us to preach to the people and to testify that he is the one appointed by God to be judge of the living and the dead.

43 To him all the prophets bear witness that everyone who believes in him receives forgiveness of sins through his name."

44 While Peter was still saying these things, the Holy Spirit fell on all who heard the word.

Peter heard Jesus teach about how the Law of Moses, the Prophets and the Psalms speak about him and so declared that all the prophets in the Old Testament talk about Jesus.

Father,

I pray for your people.

I thank you that they value the Law, read the Prophets and use the Psalms to pray and worship you.

I pray that as they read and hear your Word, your Holy Spirit will fall upon them so that the eyes of their minds and their hearts may be enlightened so that they may see Jesus and believe in him and receive forgiveness and the promise of the Comforter, the Holy Spirit.

Father,
Send your spirit afresh onto your people.

Father,
They need your Spirit to see Jesus.

Father,
They need your Spirit to believe in Jesus.

Father,
They need your Spirit to receive Jesus.

Father,
They need your Spirit to confess Jesus as their Lord and their Saviour.

Amen

Day 20

> ### Isaiah 40:28-31
>
> [28] Have you not known? Have you not heard? The LORD is the everlasting God, the Creator of the ends of the earth. He does not faint or grow weary; his understanding is unsearchable.
>
> [29] He gives power to the faint, and to him who has no might he increases strength.
>
> [30] Even youths shall faint and be weary, and young men shall fall exhausted;
>
> [31] but they who wait for the LORD shall renew their strength; they shall mount up with wings like eagles; they shall run and not be weary; they shall walk and not faint.

Father,

I praise you because you are:

the God of Israel,

the Father of your people,

the Shepherd of your flock,

their Everlasting Eternal God,

the Creator of the heavens and the earth.

Father,

I praise you because,

you do not need sleep,

you do not need to faint,

you do not need to grow weary,

you meet all our needs.

Father,

I thank you that you are always there for your family.

Father,

To those who are dying in your family welcome them with joy into your heavenly kingdom.

To those who are unsure of their faith reveal yourself to them as their Lord.

To those who are in want provide for them.

To those who grow faint give power.

To those who grow weary give courage.

To those who are lost, help them to find you and themselves.

Father,

I pray that your nation and all your people will wait on you, believe on you, hope in you, so that they may be strengthened and renewed so that:

They may mount up on the wings of your Spirit like eagles.

They shall run the race of faith set before them and not be weary.

They shall walk in your ways and not faint.

Father,
I pray in your name after whom your family is named.

Amen

Day 21

Isaiah 43:1-7

[1] But now thus says the LORD, he who created you, O Jacob, he who formed you, O Israel: "Fear not, for I have redeemed you; I have called you by name, you are mine.

[2] When you pass through the waters, I will be with you; and through the rivers, they shall not overwhelm you; when you walk through fire you shall not be burned, and the flame shall not consume you.

[3] For I am the LORD your God, the Holy One of Israel, your Savior. I give Egypt as your ransom, Cush and Seba in exchange for you.

[4] Because you are precious in my eyes, and honored, and I love you, I give men in return for you, peoples in exchange for your life.

[5] Fear not, for I am with you; I will bring your offspring from the east, and from the west I will gather you.

[6] I will say to the north, Give up, and to the south, Do not withhold; bring my sons from afar and my daughters from the end of the earth,

[7] everyone who is called by my name, whom I created for my glory, whom I formed and made."

Father,

your nation, Israel, did not come into being by accident.
It was through men such as Moses and Abraham but
Israel was called, created and formed by you for a
purpose.

To fill the earth with the knowledge of you and to
manifest your Glory.

To be your light to all other nations on the earth.

To be a blessed nation and so be a blessing to all other
nations on the earth.

Father,

I pray for all Jews who are afraid.

I pray for your people that are full of fear this day
because they are living.

In fear of persecution.

In fear of the spirit of anti-Semitism rising up against
them.

In fear of war.

In fear of what is happening to them as a nation.

In fear of what is happening to their families.

In fear of life.

In fear of death.

I pray that each one will look to you as their Saviour
and have the revelation and knowledge ,

that you are their redeemer,

that you have chosen them,

that they are special in your sight,

that you are with them,
that you love them,
that they are precious to you,
that you have not forsaken them.

I pray that they will experience your peace so that they are not afraid of what is happening because they know that as they pass through the 'waters', the 'rivers' and the 'fire' they are not alone but you are with them.
So that they will not be overwhelmed.
So that they will not be burned.
So that they will not be consumed.

Father,
I pray that you will gather all Jews back to yourself as well as calling them back to their home land.

Father,
May your Glory rest upon them as your people as it rested upon the Tabernacle in the life and leadership of Moses and also in the Temple during the life and reign of King Solomon.

Amen

Day 22

Galatians 3:23-26

23 Now before faith came, we were held captive under the law, imprisoned until the coming faith would be revealed.

24 So then, the law was our guardian until Christ came, in order that we might be justified by faith.

25 But now that faith has come, we are no longer under a guardian,

26 for in Christ Jesus you are all sons of God, through faith.

Father,

The saints in the Old Testament such as Moses and David were held captive by the Law. Even saints in the New Testament like John the Baptist were held captive by the Law until Jesus was revealed at the Jordan River when he was baptised. But now, through Jesus, those saints are justified by faith and are also your sons as Jesus is.

Father,

I thank you for the Old Testament which contains the Law, the Prophets and the Writings.

I thank you that your people today are still people of your Word and desire to live by the Law, the Prophets and the Writings.

Father,
your Law is to bring your people to your Messiah, to your Son, to Jesus.

Father,
I pray that:
As your people follow the Law, may your people have the revelation that they are following Jesus.
As your people read the Writings, may they understand that they are reading about Jesus.
As your people explore the Prophets, may they be given the knowledge that they are exploring Jesus.

Father,
your servant Paul who wrote those words to the church at Galatia was one of the greatest Jews that ever lived. I pray that you will reveal yourself to your people as you did to Paul so that they may serve you as Paul did and carry the Good News of the Gospel which is in the law to all peoples and to all nations of the world.

Amen.

Day 23

Psalms 122:1-9

1 A Song of Ascents. Of David. I was glad when they said to me, "Let us go to the house of the LORD!"

2 Our feet have been standing within your gates, O Jerusalem!

3 Jerusalem—built as a city that is bound firmly together,

4 to which the tribes go up, the tribes of the LORD, as was decreed for Israel, to give thanks to the name of the LORD.

5 There thrones for judgment were set, the thrones of the house of David.

6 Pray for the peace of Jerusalem! "May they be secure who love you!

7 Peace be within your walls and security within your towers!"

8 For my brothers and companions' sake I will say, "Peace be within you!"

9 For the sake of the house of the LORD our God, I will seek your good.

King David said in verse 3:

Jerusalem—built as a city that is bound firmly together,

The Jews believe that their capital city on this earth, the earthly Jerusalem, is a mirror image of the city in heaven, the heavenly Jerusalem. The name Jerusalem in English is a singular noun but in Hebrew the 'em' at the end of the word means the Hebrew is plural – Jersualems. The Jews believe the two Jersualems are built closely together, one on top of the other, one above and one below.

Praying for the Peace or the Shalom of Jerusalem also includes praying for the wholeness, the oneness, the unity between these two cities.

Father,
I pray that the spirit of the heavenly Jerusalem will rule and dominate the spirit of the earthly Jerusalem.

Father,
I pray that your will, which is done perfectly in the Jerusalem above, will also be done perfectly in the Jerusalem below.

Father,
I pray that your glory which fills, rests upon and resides in the heavenly Jerusalem will also fill, rest upon and reside in the earthly Jerusalem.

Genesis 28:11-17

[11] And he came to a certain place and stayed there that night, because the sun had set. Taking one of the stones of the place, he put it under his head and lay down in that place to sleep.

[12] And he dreamed, and behold, there was a ladder set up on the earth, and the top of it reached to heaven. And behold, the angels of God were ascending and descending on it!

[13] And behold, the LORD stood above it and said, "I am the LORD, the God of Abraham your father and the God of Isaac. The land on which you lie I will give to you and to your offspring.

[14] your offspring shall be like the dust of the earth, and you shall spread abroad to the west and to the east and to the north and to the south, and in you and your offspring shall all the families of the earth be blessed.

[15] Behold, I am with you and will keep you wherever you go, and will bring you back to this land. For I will not leave you until I have done what I have promised you."

[16] Then Jacob awoke from his sleep and said,

> "Surely the LORD is in this place, and I did not know it."
>
> [17] And he was afraid and said, "How awesome is this place! This is none other than the house of God, and this is the gate of heaven."

The Stone Edition are a set of Jewish Commentaries on the Old Testament and they say that when Jacob was running from his brother he slept the night on the mountains of Jerusalem, Mount Moriah, where Abraham sacrificed Isaac, where the Temple was built. This is the same area where Jesus was crucified. Jews believe that Jacob had found the Jerusalem below which was the gateway to the one above.

Father,

I pray that your people will see Jerusalem as their gateway to you.

I pray that in that city they will meet with you, fellowship with you, worship you and be the people you have called them to be.

Father,

Open the eyes of their hearts so that they.

May know your presence.

May know your promises.

May be focused on your eternal city and it's King, Jesus.

Amen

Day 24

Ephesians 1:16-18

[16] I do not cease to give thanks for you, remembering you in my prayers,

[17] that the God of our Lord Jesus Christ, the Father of glory, may give you the Spirit of wisdom and of revelation in the knowledge of him,

[18] having the eyes of your hearts enlightened, that you may know what is the hope to which he has called you.

Father,

I thank you for Israel.

I thank you for your people.

I thank you that you chose your people out of all the nations of the world.

I thank you that you chose the land of Israel out of all the lands of the world.

I thank you that your Son loves your people, they are also his people.

I thank you that your Son freed your people from their sins by his own blood.

Father,

Bless your people with your Spirit so that they may understand what Jesus has done for them.

Bless your people with your Spirit so that they may understand the freedom he died to bring to them.

Father,

I thank you that you gave to your people the Old Testament scriptures.

Father,

I pray that your Holy Spirit will enlighten the hearts of your people so that whenever they read the Old Testament they will have their eyes opened and will see Jesus.

That they will read and have the revelation that the prophecies about the Messiah apply to him.

I pray that as they read through their scriptures they may see the revelations and understand ,

the mystery of the Kingdom of God,

the mystery of the church, the Messiah's people,

the mystery of the cross.

Let your people see what their Messiah saw as he read, studied and meditated the Old Testament when he walked this earth.

Let your people see what your Son was revealing to his disciples as he taught them from the Old Testament scriptures about Himself.

Amen

Day 25

Matthew 23:37

[37] O Jerusalem, Jerusalem, the city that kills the prophets and stones those who are sent to it! How often would I have gathered your children together as a hen gathers her brood under her wings, and you were not willing!

Father,

This reveals your heart towards your people.

Despite their rejection of your prophets.

Despite their rejection of your own Son,

you still want to demonstrate your love to them.

As a hen gathers her chicks under her wings so you wanted to gather your people under the shadow of your wings and you still want to.

Father,

This is not only your heart but also the heart of your Son, the one they not only rejected but crucified.

Matthew 9:36

36 When he saw the crowds, he had compassion for them, because they were harassed and helpless, like sheep without a shepherd.

Matthew 14:14

14 When he went ashore he saw a great crowd, and he had compassion on them and healed their sick.

Matthew 15:32

32 Then Jesus called his disciples to him and said, "I have compassion on the crowd because they have been with me now three days and have nothing to eat. And I am unwilling to send them away hungry, lest they faint on the way."

Father,
Give me your heart towards your people.

Jesus,
Give me your compassion towards your people.

Jesus, your compassion wanted to gather your people together and to love them, to shepherd them, to care for them, to guide them, to reveal the Father's heart to them.

Jesus,
We thank you that you do not change and you still love your people.

Father,
We thank you that you do not change and still love your children, your chosen ones.

Father,
Send your Spirit onto your people so that they are no longer a nation that 'would not' but a nation that 'does'.

Holy Spirit,
Turn the hearts of God's children back to him.
Holy Spirit,
Turn the hearts of God's children to His Son, their long-promised Redeemer and Messiah.

Matthew 9:37-38

[37] Then he said to his disciples, "The harvest is plentiful, but the laborers are few;
[38] therefore pray earnestly to the Lord of the harvest to send out laborers into his harvest."

Father, Jesus, Holy Spirit.

I pray,

Let not one of your people be lost.

Let not one of your people fail to be gathered into your arms in this life.

Let not one of your people fail to live for eternity in your arms.

Amen

Day 26

1 John 4:7-12

[7] Beloved, let us love one another, for love is from God, and whoever loves has been born of God and knows God.

[8] Anyone who does not love does not know God, because God is love.

[9] In this the love of God was made manifest among us, that God sent his only Son into the world, so that we might live through him.

[10] In this is love, not that we have loved God but that he loved us and sent his Son to be the propitiation for our sins.

[11] Beloved, if God so loved us, we also ought to love one another.

[12] No one has ever seen God; if we love one another, God abides in us and his love is perfected in us.

> **1 John 4:19-21**
>
> [19] We love because he first loved us.
>
> [20] If anyone says, "I love God," and hates his brother, he is a liar; for he who does not love his brother whom he has seen cannot love God whom he has not seen.
>
> [21] And this commandment we have from him: whoever loves God must also love his brother.

These words were written by the Apostle John to the body of Christ, the church. Yes, we are to love all who are part of the body of Christ, and as we meditate on the words of Jesus and the other letters to the church in the New Testament we realise that we are also to love all people everywhere and this includes God's chosen people, the Jews.

Father,
I ask forgiveness that your people have not always been treated with love by the church and Christians.
I ask forgiveness for all those acts against your people in which the church and Christians were involved that caused your people to experience hardship, persecution and even death rather than love.

Father,

I pray that you will heal the hearts of your people so that they are able to forgive Christians and to forgive the church for not displaying unconditional love to your people.

Father,

May the sign of the Cross become a sign of salvation to your people as it is to the church rather than the sign and memory of their persecutors.

Father,

I pray that you will anoint your church with your love, divine love, so that Christians and the church will love your people.

May that love be manifested so that your people experience love, are surprised by that love and are drawn to that love and so discover the truth about Christians, the church and Jesus.

Amen

Day 27

> **Ephesians 2:12**
>
> 12 ...remember that you were at that time separated from Christ, alienated from the commonwealth of Israel and strangers to the covenants of promise, having no hope and without God in the world.

Father,

When Paul wrote these words, he was talking to Gentiles who became part of the church.

He was talking about what the Jews; his people and your people had and still have.

They have the promise of the coming Messiah.

They are a nation founded by you.

They have Covenants of Promise.

They have hope in this world and the next.

They have you in this world, here and now.

Father,

your people are so blessed and are so rich.

May they understand that their Messiah has come and will come again.

May they have the revelation that their Messiah is your Son, Jesus.

Father,

your people are so blessed and are so rich.

May the government of Israel rest on the shoulders of
your Son so that he may rule and reign as their King.

Father,

your people are so blessed and are so rich.

May they understand afresh the Covenants of Promise
you have with them and live by them and be victorious
and blessed through them.

Father,

your people are so blessed and are so rich.

May they understand the hope to which you have called
them.

Father,

your people are so blessed and are so rich.

May they continue to decree and declare Psalms 91:2 ;

*My refuge and my fortress, my God, in whom I
trust.*

Amen

Day 28

Joel 2:28-29

28 And it shall come to pass afterward, that I will pour out my Spirit on all flesh; your sons and your daughters shall prophesy, your old men shall dream dreams, and your young men shall see visions.

29Even on the male and female servants in those days I will pour out my Spirit.

Father,

Pour out your Holy Spirit onto your people.

Pour out your Holy Spirit onto your people who live in Israel and onto your people who live amongst the nations.

Father,

May your children prophesy about the goodness and mercy you show your children.

May your children have dreams about your Glory upon them and your greatness in their lives.

May your children have visions of their future and their destiny in your will and in your Kingdom.

May your children experience the presence, the person and the power of your Holy Spirit in their lives.

Holy Spirit,

Break the yoke of the law of sin and death that is upon their lives.

Free them from that law so that they may live under your Holy Spirit, the law of the Spirit of life.

Holy Spirit,

manifest yourself in their lives in:

Wisdom.

Understanding.

Counsel.

Might.

Knowledge.

Fear of the Lord.

Holy Spirit,

manifest yourself in their lives as:

Love.

Joy.

Peace.

Longsuffering.

Kindness.

Goodness.

Faithfulness.

Gentleness.

Self-control.

Holy Spirit.

Anoint all Jews everywhere in the Name of Jesus.

Amen

Day 29

Revelation 7:1-8

1 After this I saw four angels standing at the four corners of the earth, holding back the four winds of the earth, that no wind might blow on earth or sea or against any tree.

2 Then I saw another angel ascending from the rising of the sun, with the seal of the living God, and he called with a loud voice to the four angels who had been given power to harm earth and sea, 3 saying, "Do not harm the earth or the sea or the trees, until we have sealed the servants of our God on their foreheads."

4 And I heard the number of the sealed, 144,000, sealed from every tribe of the sons of Israel:

5 12,000 from the tribe of Judah were sealed, 12,000 from the tribe of Reuben, 12,000 from the tribe of Gad,

6 12,000 from the tribe of Asher, 12,000 from the tribe of Naphtali, 12,000 from the tribe of Manasseh,

7 12,000 from the tribe of Simeon, 12,000 from the tribe of Levi, 12,000 from the tribe of Issachar,

8 12,000 from the tribe of Zebulun, 12,000 from the tribe of Joseph, 12,000 from the tribe of Benjamin were sealed.

The Apostle John saw that at the end of times God will set a seal on his servants who many believe are the chosen Jews who will form his army of end time evangelists.

Father,
Prepare your people for:
The return of Jesus.
The judgement of the nations.
The end of this age.

Father,
Prepare your people to be your servants so that once again they may serve you by:
Being a light to the nations.
Seeking to establish your Heavenly Kingdom on this earth.
Seeking to ensure your will is done in this world.
Proclaiming your name to the world.
Serving and saving the nations of this world as their Messiah did.

Father,
Seal and protect those of your people you have chosen to represent you in the last days.

Father,
Empower them and equip them for their calling and their ministry.

Father,

May they as your servants declare that,

you are their God,

you are their Refuge,

you are their Fortress.

In you they trust.

So that they will be victorious in their stand for you and with you in the end of times.

Amen

Day 30

> **Ezekiel 11:16-17**
>
> 16 Therefore say, 'Thus says the Lord GOD: Though I removed them far off among the nations, and though I scattered them among the countries, yet I have been a sanctuary to them for a while in the countries where they have gone.'
>
> 17 Therefore say, 'Thus says the Lord GOD: I will gather you from the peoples and assemble you out of the countries where you have been scattered, and I will give you the land of Israel.'

Father,

you promised your people that you would be a sanctuary to them whilst you took them away from their Land and scattered them throughout the nations of the world.

Father,

you promised your people that you would gather them from where they had been scattered back to their Land, the Land you had given them.

Father,

Thank you that you are faithful to keep your promises.

Father,

Thank you that you have throughout the ages been a faithful sanctuary to your people. Throughout history you have always provided a sanctuary when there was no peace.

Father,

Thank you that you are now calling your people back home, back to Israel.

Father,

If any of your people have strayed from you like lost sheep then seek them out as the Good Shepherd of Israel and carry them home.

Amen, Father, Amen.

Saturday

> **Deuteronomy 5:12-15**
>
> 12 Observe the Sabbath day, to keep it holy, as the LORD your God commanded you.
>
> 13 Six days you shall labor and do all your work, 14 but the seventh day is a Sabbath to the LORD your God. On it you shall not do any work, you or your son or your daughter or your male servant or your female servant, or your ox or your donkey or any of your livestock, or the sojourner who is within your gates, that your male servant and your female servant may rest as well as you.
>
> 15 you shall remember that you were a slave in the land of Egypt, and the LORD your God brought you out from there with a mighty hand and an outstretched arm. Therefore the LORD your God commanded you to keep the Sabbath day.

Saturday is the Holy Day for Jews. It is their Sabbath Day. Sabbath means to rest, to cease from work.

The Jews have a poem where the Sabbath is personified as a bride who visits her husband, Israel. Some of the lines of the poem are:

Come my friend to meet the bride; let us welcome the presence of the bride.

Come, let us go to meet the Sabbath, for it is a well-spring of blessing.

Come in peace, thou crown of thy husband, with rejoicing and with cheerfulness, in the midst of the faithful of the chosen people; come O bride, come O bride.

Father,
May your people honour this Sabbath day.
May they rest from life and all its business and responsibilities.
May they focus on you, their Creator, their Caller, their True Husband.

Father,
May this day be a day of blessing and refreshment for your people.
May this day be a day of celebration and rejoicing for them before you.
Amen

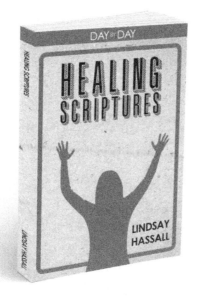

Day by Day: Healing Scriptures
by Lindsay Hassall
ISBN: 978-0-9932090-9-3
78 pages
Paperback
RRP: UK: £6.95 USA: $9.00
www.GileadBooksPublishing.com

Printed in Great Britain
by Amazon